Kantjil

A tale from Indonesia
retold by Cathy Spagnoli
Illustrations by Fabricio Vanden Broeck

Kantjil, the clever little mouse-deer, was resting in the sun when SUDDENLY he heard his enemy, Tiger, close by.

"I can't outrun Tiger now," thought Kantjil, "so I'd better outthink him."

He turned his head,
saw a big, white rock,
and knew what to do.

Quickly, he picked up a banana leaf and stood near the rock.

As Tiger bounded into the clearing, Kantjil slowly, carefully fanned the rock.

"KANTJIL!" roared Tiger. "WHAT ARE YOU DOING?"

But Kantjil just ignored Tiger and kept on fanning and fanning.

"You little monkey, answer me!" Tiger growled.

"Silly striped bully, figure it out for yourself!" replied Kantjil, looking bored but shaking inside.

"KANTJIL, TELL ME NOW BEFORE I CHEW YOU UP!" ordered Tiger.

"All right. All right." replied Kantjil.
"The great Nabi Sulaiman has given me the important task of guarding his favorite cake."

"What kind of cake is it, Kantjil?" asked Tiger, staring at the rock. "And why didn't he ask ME to guard it?"

"It's a special steamed rice cake. And he didn't ask YOU because you're BIG, but NOT SMART. I am little but I have a LARGE BRAIN," bragged Kantjil, "so I am to guard ALL of his forest treasures."

Tiger glared and opened his mouth.

"Well, then, I'll just take a bite, and YOUR BRAIN CAN TRY TO STOP ME!" he roared.

"Tiger, Tiger," said Kantjil, sighing, "if you want to eat it, I can't stop you. YET I MUST WARN YOU that if anyone but Nabi Sulaiman eats it, this soft sweet will taste like a rock, not a cake."

"I'll still try it," growled Tiger. He hung out his tongue.

"Fine, Tiger," said Kantjil, "but if it breaks your teeth, it's your own fault for not listening. I'll go over there, and then I won't see you. Later, I can truthfully tell Nabi Sulaiman that I didn't see ANYONE eat HIS cake."

"Thank you, Kantjil," said Tiger.

Kantjil moved quickly into the trees as Tiger bit into the rock.

"OO-OO-OOOOOOOOOOOOO!"

Tiger's roar of pain flew through the trees, following Kantjil as he raced away.

Tiger, his teeth tender, his mouth sore,
soon followed that roar, FURIOUS at the mouse-deer.
Kantjil, hearing Tiger close behind,
knew that only another trick would save him.

Just then, Kantjil saw a monstrous snake sleeping in a field.

He went up and ve-ry, ve-ry care-ful-ly sat on the snake, just as Tiger came racing up.

"TIGER! WAIT! Don't step on the belt of Nabi Sulaiman!" called Kantjil.

Tiger stopped and stared at the snake.

"Are you lying again, you mealy mouse-deer?" asked Tiger. "Is that really Nabi Sulaiman's belt?"

"Yes, it is his BEST belt, Tiger," replied Kantjil. "He will wear it tonight to a grand feast. It looks most splendid wrapped around his waist."

"It does seem soft, like silk," said Tiger. "I want to try it on."

"Tiger, you are asking for trouble again," warned Kantjil. "If anyone but Nabi Sulaiman wears this belt, it turns into a snake. Do not take a chance."

"I must. I will," said the stubborn tiger.

"All right," said Kantjil.
"I told you of the danger.
Now I will hide my eyes."
And he hopped off into the trees.

Tiger picked up the snake and started to wrap it around himself.

But the snake awoke and was MOST annoyed. He started to squeeze
and sque-e-eze
and sque-e-e-eze poor Tiger, who could hardly breathe.

"Heh-eh-eh-elp!" gasped Tiger.

He crashed against nearby trees, trying to break the snake's grip.

At last, the snake dropped off and slithered away.

Then Tiger limped painfully on, searching for Kantjil.

Kantjil, meanwhile, had found a tree next to a clump of bamboo. In the tree he found a hole,
crawled into it,
and was soon asleep.

When Tiger came up and saw Kantjil snoring, he roared, "KANTJIL, YOU'VE TRICKED ME TWICE TODAY! THIS TIME, YOU WON'T ESCAPE!"

Kantjil rubbed his big eyes, stretched his tiny legs, and thought quickly.

"Tiger," he said, "I told you the truth about Nabi Sulaiman's cake and belt. You didn't believe me, and you were hurt. So I won't tell you anything about the trumpet of Nabi Sulaiman."

"What trumpet, Kantjil?" asked Tiger.

Kantjil pointed to the bamboo swaying.

"Here it is, ready for playing whenever Nabi Sulaiman wants," he said. "What a marvelous sound it makes, Tiger."

"Kantjil, I'm sorry I was angry with you. Now let's be friends, and let me try Nabi Sulaiman's trumpet," begged Tiger.

"No, Tiger, I can't," said Kantjil.

"PLEASE, *PLEASE,* Kantjil," pleaded Tiger.

"Well...all right. Come up here carefully," said Kantjil. So Tiger climbed up into Kantjil's hole.

"Now, Tiger," said Kantjil, "I'll go down and call the wind."

Then Kantjil gave Tiger a piece of bamboo that was split at one end.

"Put your tongue in this crack and hold the trumpet tightly," Kantjil told him. "When the wind blows, the trumpet will sound with a roar."

Tiger agreed, and Kantjil scampered down.

Tiger slipped his tongue into the crack and waited eagerly for a breeze.

Kantjil waved his hooves for wind while moving farther and farther away.

Suddenly,
the wind blew,
the bamboo shook,
and poor Tiger's tongue
was pinched harder
and harder
and harder.

"AAAOOOOOOOOWWWW!"
trumpeted Tiger in the greatest of pain.
He struggled to free his tongue,
but the bamboo only held it tighter
as the wind blew
and blew
and blew.

Finally, the wind calmed, and Tiger slo-o-o-owly, gently eased his tongue out.

Then he raced off in a rage to find Kantjil!

But by that time, Kantjil was safely back in his home, far, far away.